Objections to Astrology

Objections to Astrology

with articles by

Bart J. Bok
and
Lawrence E. Jerome

PB *Prometheus Books*
BUFFALO, N.Y. 14215

Reprinted from *The Humanist* 35, no. 5 (September/October 1975) with permission:

"Objections to Astrology"
"A Critical Look at Astrology," by Bart J. Bok
"Astrology: Magic or Science?" by Lawrence E. Jerome

Published 1975 by Prometheus Books
923 Kensington Avenue, Buffalo, New York 14215

Library of Congress Number 75-29798
ISBN 0-87975-059-6

Printed in the United States of America

Contents

Objections to Astrology

Objections to Astrology

A Statement by 192 Leading Scientists

Scientists in a variety of fields have become concerned about the increased acceptance of astrology in many parts of the world. We, the undersigned—astronomers, astrophysicists, and scientists in other fields—wish to caution the public against the unquestioning acceptance of the predictions and advice given privately and publicly by astrologers. Those who wish to believe in astrology should realize that there is no scientific foundation for its tenets.

In ancient times people believed in the predictions and advice of astrologers because astrology was part and parcel of their magical world view. They looked upon celestial objects as abodes or omens of the Gods and thus intimately connected with events here on earth; they had no concept of the vast distances from the earth to the planets and stars. Now that these distances can and have been calculated, we can see how infinitesimally small are the gravitational and other effects produced by the distant planets and the far more distant stars. It is simply a mistake to imagine that the forces exerted by stars and planets at the moment of birth can in any way shape our futures. Neither is it true that the position of distant heavenly bodies makes certain days or periods more favorable to particular of kinds of action, or that the sign under which one was born determines one's compatibility or incompatibility with other people.

Why do people believe in astrology? In these uncertain times many long for the comfort of having guidance in making decisions. They would like to believe in a destiny predetermined by astral forces beyond their control. However, we must all face the world, and we must realize that our futures lie in ourselves, and not in the stars.

One would imagine, in this day of widespread enlightenment and education, that it would be unnecessary to debunk beliefs based on magic and superstition. Yet, acceptance of astrology pervades modern society. We are especially disturbed by the continued uncritical dissemination of astrological charts, forecasts, and horoscopes by the media and by otherwise reputable newspapers, magazines, and book publishers. This can only contribute to the growth of irrationalism and obscurantism. We believe that the time has come to challenge directly and forcefully the pretentious claims of astrological charlatans.

It should be apparent that those individuals who continue to have faith in astrology do so in spite of the fact that there is no verified scientific basis for their beliefs, and indeed that there is strong evidence to the contrary.

Bart J. Bok, *emeritus*
professor of astronomy
University of Arizona

Lawrence E. Jerome
science writer
Santa Clara, California

Paul Kurtz
professor of philosophy
SUNY at Buffalo

Signers

NOBEL PRIZE WINNERS

Hans A. Bethe, *professor emeritus of physics, Cornell*
Sir Francis Crick, *Medical Research Council, Cambridge, Eng.*
Sir John Eccles, *distinguished professor of physiology and biophysics, SUNY at Buffalo*
Gerhard Herzberg, *distinguished research scientist, National Research Council of Canada*
Wassily Leontief, *professor of economics, Harvard University*
Konrad Lorenz, *univ. prof., Austrian Academy of Sciences*
André M. Lwoff, *honorary professor, Institut Pasteur, Paris*
Sir Peter Medawar, *Medical Research Council, Middlesex, Eng.*
Jacques Monod, *Institut Pasteur, Paris*
Robert S. Mulliken, *dist. prof. of chemistry, Univ. of Chicago*
Linus C. Pauling, *professor of chemistry, Stanford University*
Edward M. Purcell, *Gerhard Gade univ. prof., Harvard Univ.*
Paul A. Samuelson, *professor of economics, MIT*
Julian Schwinger, *professor of physics, U. of Calif., Los Angeles*
Glenn T. Seaborg, *univ. professor, Univ. of Calif., Berkeley*
J. Tinbergen, *professor emeritus, Rotterdam, The Netherlands*
N. Tinbergen, *emer. professor of animal behavior, Oxford Univ.*
Harold C. Urey, *professor emeritus, Univ. of Calif., San Diego*
George Wald, *professor of biology, Harvard University*

George O. Abell, *chmn., Dept. of Astron., U. of Cal., Los Angeles*
Lawrence H. Aller, *professor, Univ. of Calif., Los Angeles*
Edoardo Amaldi, *prof. of physics, University of Rome*
Richard Berendzen, *dean, Coll. of Arts and Sci., American Univ.*

William P. Bidelman, *professor, Case Western Reserve Univ.*
Jacob Bigeleisen, *professor, University of Rochester*
D. Scott Birney, *prof. of astronomy, Wellesley College*
Karl-Heinz Böhm, *professor, University of Washington*
Lyle B. Borst, *prof. of physics and astronomy, SUNY at Buffalo*
Peter B. Boyce, *staff astronomer, Lowell Observatory*
Harvey Brooks, *prof. of technology and public policy, Harvard*
William Buscombe, *prof. of astronomy, Northwestern Univ.*
Eugene R. Capriotti, *prof. of astronomy, Ohio State Univ.*
H. E. Carter, *coord. of interdisciplinary programs, U. of Arizona*
J. W. Chamberlain, *prof. of astronomy, Rice University*
Von Del Chamberlain, *Smithsonian Institution*
S. Chandrasekhar, *prof. of astronomy, Univ. of Chicago*
Mark R. Chartrand III, *chmn., Hayden Planetarium*
Hong-Yee Chiu, *NASA*
Preston Cloud, *prof. of geology, U. of Cal., Santa Barbara*
Peter S. Conti, *prof. of astrophysics, Univ. of Colorado*
Allan F. Cook II, *astrophysicist, Smithsonian Observatory*
Alan Cottrell, *master, Jesus College, Cambridge, England*
Bryce Crawford, Jr., *prof. of chemistry, Univ. of Minnesota*
David D. Cudaback, *research astronomer, Univ. of Calif., Berkeley*
A. Dalgarno, *prof. of astronomy, Harvard*
Hallowell Davis, *Central Inst. for the Deaf, Univ. City, Mo.*
Morris S. Davis, *prof. of astronomy, Univ. of No. Carolina*
Peter van de Kamp, *director emeritus, Sproul Observatory*
A. H. Delsemme, *prof. of astrophysics, Univ. of Toledo*
Robert H. Dicke, *Albert Einstein prof. of science, Princeton*
Bertram Donn, *head, Astrochemical Branch, Goddard Space Center, NASA*
Paul Doty, *prof. of biochemistry, Harvard*
Frank D. Drake, *dir., Natl. Astron. and Ionosphere Ctr., Cornell*

Lee A. DuBridge, *pres. emeritus, Calif. Inst. of Technology*
Harold Edgerton, *professor, MIT*
H. K. Eichhorn-von Wurmb, *chmn., Dept. of Astron., Univ. of South Florida*
R. M. Emberson, *dir., Tech. Services Inst. of Electrical and Electronics Engineers*
Howard W. Emmons, *professor of mechanical engineering, Harvard*
Eugene E. Epstein, *staff scientist, The Aerospace Corp.*
Henry Eyring, *distinguished prof. of chemistry, Univ. of Utah*
Charles A. Federer, Jr., *president, Sky Pub. Corp.*
Robert Fleischer, *Astronomy Section, National Science Foundation.*
Henry F. Fliegel, *technical staff, Jet Propulsion Laboratory*
William A. Fowler, *institute prof. of physics, Calif. Inst. of Tech.*
Fred A. Franklin, *astronomer, Smithsonian Astrophysical Observatory*
Laurence W. Fredrick, *prof. of astronomy, U. of Virginia*
Tom Gehrels, *Lunar and Planetary Lab., Univ. of Arizona*
Riccardo Giacconi, *Center for Astrophysics, Cambridge, Mass.*
Owen Gingerich, *prof. of astronomy, Harvard*
Thomas Gold, *professor, Cornell*
Leo Goldberg, *director, Kitt Peak National Observatory*
Maurice Goldhaber, *Brookhaven National Laboratory*
Mark A. Gordon, *Natl. Radio Astronomy Observatory*
Jesse L. Greenstein, *prof. of astrophysics, Cal. Inst. of Tech.*
Kenneth Greisen, *prof. of physics, Cornell*
Howard D. Greyber, *consultant, Potomac, Md.*
Herbert Gursky, *astrophysicist, Smithsonian Institution*
John P. Hagen, *chmn., Dept. of Astronomy, Penn. State Univ.*
Philip Handler, *president, National Academy of Sciences*
William K. Hartmann, *Planetary Science Inst., Tucson, Arizona*

Leland J. Haworth, *spec. assist. to the pres., Associated Univs.*
Carl Heiles, *prof. of astronomy, U. of Cal., Berkeley*
A. Heiser, *director, Dyer Observatory, Vanderbilt University*
H. L. Helfer, *prof. of astronomy, Univ. of Rochester*
George H. Herbig, *astronomer, Lick Observatory, U. of Cal.*
Arthur A. Hoag, *astronomer, Kitt Peak Natl. Observatory*
Paul W. Hodge, *prof. of astronomy, Univ. of Washington*
Dorrit Hoffleit, *director, Maria Mitchell Observatory*
William E. Howard III, *Natl. Radio Astronomy Observatory*
Nancy Houk, *Dept. of Astronomy, Univ. of Michigan*
Fred Hoyle, *fellow, St. Johns College, Cambridge Univ.*
Icko Iben, Jr., *chmn., Dept. of Astronomy, U. of Illinois*
John T. Jefferies, *director, Inst. for Astronomy, U. of Hawaii*
Frank C. Jettner, *Dept. of Astronomy, SUNY at Albany*
J. R. Jokipii, *prof. of planetary sciences, Univ. of Arizona*
Joost H. Kiewiet de Jonge, *assoc. prof. of astron., U. of Pittsburgh*
Kenneth Kellermann, *Nat. Radio Astronomy Observatory*
Ivan R. King, *prof. of astron., U. of Cal., Berkeley*
Rudolf Kompfner, *professor emeritus, Stanford University*
William S. Kovach, *staff scientist, General Dynamics/Convair*
M. R. Kundu, *prof. of astronomy, Univ. of Maryland*
Lewis Larmore, *dir. of tech., Office of Naval Research*
Kam-Ching Leung, *dir., Behlen Observatory, Univ. of Nebraska*
I. M. Levitt, *dir. emer., Fels Planetarium of Franklin Institute*
C. C. Lin, *professor, MIT*
Albert P. Linnell, *professor, Michigan State Univ.*
M. Stanley Livingston, *Dept. of Physics, MIT*
Frank J. Low, *research prof., University of Arizona*
Willem J. Luyten, *University of Minnesota*
Richard E. McCrosky, *Smithsonian Astrophysical Observatory*
W. D. McElroy, *Univ. of Calif., San Diego*
Carl S. Marvel, *prof. of chemistry, Univ. of Arizona*

Margaret W. Mayall, *consul., Am. Assoc. of Variable Star Obser.*
Nicholas U. Mayall, *former dir., Kitt Peak Natl. Observatory*
Donald H. Menzel, *former director, Harvard College Observatory*
Alfred H. Mikesell, *Kitt Peak Natl. Observatory*
Freeman D. Miller, *prof. of astronomy, Univ. of Michigan*
Alan T. Moffet, *prof. of radio astron., Calif. Inst. of Technology*
Delo E. Mook, *assist. prof. of physics and astronomy, Dartmouth*
Marston Morse, *prof. emer., Inst. for Adv. Study, Princeton*
G. F. W. Mulders, *former head, Astron. Section, NSF*
Guido Münch, *prof. of astronomy, Cal. Inst. of Technology*
Edward P. Ney, *regents prof. of astronomy, Univ. of Minn.*
J. Neyman, *director, statistical lab, Univ. of Cal., Berkeley*
C. R. O'Dell, *project scientist, Large Space Telescope, NASA*
John A. O'Keefe, *Goddard Space Flight Center, NASA*
J. H. Oort, *dir., University Observatory, Leiden, Netherlands*
Tobias C. Owen, *prof. of astronomy, SUNY at Stony Brook*
Eugene N. Parker, *professor of physics and astron., U. of Chicago*
Arno A. Penzias, *Bell Laboratories*
A. Keith Pierce, *solar astronomer, Kitt Peak National Observatory*
Daniel M. Popper, *professor of astronomy, UCLA*
Frank Press, *prof. of geophysics, MIT*
R. M. Price, *radio spectrum manager, Natl. Science Foundation*
William M. Protheroe, *prof. of astronomy, Ohio State University*
John D. G. Rather, *Dept. of Astronomy, Univ. of Calif., Irvine*
Robert S. Richardson, *former assoc. dir., Griffith Observatory*
A. Marguerite Risley, *prof. emer., Randolph-Macon College*
Franklin E. Roach, *astronomer, Honolulu, Hawaii*
Walter Orr Roberts, *Aspen Inst. for Humanistic Studies*
William W. Roberts, Jr., *associate prof., University of Virginia*
R. N. Robertson, *Australian National University*
James P. Rodman, *prof. of astronomy, Mt. Union College*

Bruno Rossi, *prof. emeritus, MIT*
E. E. Salpeter, *professor, Cornell University*
Gertrude Scharff-Goldhaber, *physicist, Brookhaven Natl. Lab.*
John D. Schopp, *prof. of astronomy, San Diego State University*
Julian J. Schreur, *prof. of astronomy, Valdosta State College*
E. L. Scott, *professor, University of California, Berkeley*
Frederick Seitz, *president, The Rockefeller University*
C. D. Shane, *Lick Observatory*
Alan H. Shapley, *U.S. Dept. of Commerce, NOAA*
Frank H. Shu, *assoc. prof. of astronomy, Univ. of Cal., Berkeley*
Bancroft W. Sitterly, *prof. of physics emer., American Univ.*
Charlotte M. Sitterly, *Washington, D.C.*
B. F. Skinner, *prof. emeritus, Harvard*
Harlan J. Smith, *dir., McDonald Observ., Univ. of Texas, Austin*
Sabatino Sofia, *staff scientist, NASA*
František Šorm, *professor, Institute of Organic Chemistry, Prague, Czech.*
G. Ledyard Stebbins, *prof. emeritus, Univ. of California*
C. Bruce Stephenson, *prof. of astronomy, Case Western Reserve*
Walter H. Stockmayer, *prof. of chemistry, Dartmouth*
Marshall H. Stone, *professor, University of Massachusetts*
N. Wyman Storer, *prof. emeritus of astronomy, Univ. of Kansas*
Hans E. Suess, *prof. of geochemistry, Univ. of Cal., San Diego*
T. L. Swihart, *prof. of astronomy, Univ. of Arizona*
Pol Swings, *Institut d'Astrophysique, Esneux, Belgium*
J. Szentágothai, *Semmelweis Univ. Med. School, Budapest*
Joseph H. Taylor, Jr., *assoc. prof. of astronomy, Univ. of Mass.*
Frederick E. Terman, *vice-pres. and provost emeritus, Stanford*
Yervant Terzian, *assoc. prof. of space science, Cornell*
Patrick Thaddeus, *Inst. for Space Studies, New York, N.Y.*
Kip S. Thorne, *prof. of theor. physics, Cal. Inst. of Technology*
Charles R. Tolbert, *McCormick Observ., Charlottesville, Va.*

Alar Toomre, *prof. of applied mathematics, MIT*
Merle A. Tuve, *Carnegie Institution of Washington*
S. Vasilevskis, *emer. prof. of astronomy, Univ. of Cal., Santa Cruz*
Maurice B. Visscher, *emer. prof. of physiology, Univ. of Minn.*
Joan Vorpahl, *Aerospace Corp., Los Angeles*
Campbell M. Wade, *Natl. Radio Astronomy Observatory*
N. E. Wagman, *emer. dir., Allegheny Observatory, U. of Pittsb.*
George Wallerstein, *prof. of astronomy, Univ. of Washington*
Fred L. Whipple, *Phillips astronomer, Harvard*
Hassler Whitney, *professor, Inst. for Advanced Study, Princeton*
Adolf N. Witt, *prof. of astronomy, Univ. of Toledo*
Frank Bradshaw Wood, *prof. of astronomy, University of Florida*
Charles E. Worley, *astronomer, U.S. Naval Observatory*
Jeffries Wyman, *Instituto Regina Elena, Rome*
Chi Yuan, *assoc. prof. of physics, CCNY*

A Critical Look
at Astrology

Bart J. Bok

A Critical Look at Astrology

During the past ten years, we have witnessed an alarming increase in the spread of astrology. This pseudoscience seems to hold fascination especially for people of college age who are looking for firm guideposts in the confused world of the present. It is not surprising that people believe in astrology when most of our daily newspapers regularly carry columns about it and when some of our universities and junior colleges actually offer astrology courses. The public, young and old, has the right to expect from its scientists, especially from astronomers, clear and clarifying statements showing that astrology lacks a firm scientific foundation.

I have spoken out publicly against astrology every ten years or so, beginning in 1941 in "Scientists Look at Astrology," written with Margaret W. Mayall for the now-defunct *Scientific Monthly* (Volume 52). I have softened a bit since my early crusading days, for I have come to realize that astrology cannot be stopped by simple scientific argument only. To some it seems almost a religion. All I can do is state clearly and unequivocally that modern concepts of astronomy and space physics give no support—better said, negative support—to the tenets of astrology.

Not more than a dozen or so of my fellow astronomers have spoken out publicly on astrology. Twice I have suggested to my friends on the Council of the American Astronomical Society that the council issue a statement pointing out that there is no scientific foundation for astrological beliefs. Both times I was turned down, the principal argument being that it is below the dignity of a professional society to recognize that astrological beliefs are prevalent today. To me it seems socially and morally inexcusable for the society not to have taken a firm stand. Astronomers as a group have obviously not provided the guidance that the public sorely needs. Those who live in a free society are entitled to believe in whatever causes they care to espouse. However, I have had more than half a century of day-to-day and night-to-night contacts with the starry heavens, and it is my duty to speak up and to state clearly that I see no evidence that the stars and planets influence or control our personal lives and that I have found much evidence to the contrary.

THE ORIGINS OF ASTROLOGY

The article by Lawrence E. Jerome that follows this one shows that astrology had its origins before the birth of Christ. Present-day astrological concepts and techniques largely go back to the period 100 to 200 A.D. It was only natural that early civilizations would consider the stars and planets in the heavens as awesome evidence of supernatural powers that could magically affect their lives. Variety was brought into the picture by the constantly changing aspects of the heavens. No one can blame the Egyptians, the Greeks, the Arabs, or the people of India for having established systems of astrology at times when they were also laying the foundations for astronomy. Right up to the days of Copernicus, Galileo, and Kepler (who was an expert astrologer)—even to the time of Isaac Newton—there were good reasons for exploring astrology.

However, all this changed when the first measurements were made of the distances to the sun, planets, and stars and when the masses of these objects were determined. The foundations of astrology began to crumble when we came to realize how vanishingly small are the forces exerted by the celestial objects on things and people on earth—and how very small are the amounts of radiation associated with them received on earth. The only perceptible and observable effects evident to all of us are produced by the tidal forces caused by the gravity of the moon and sun. To assume that the sun, moon, and planets would exert special critical forces upon a baby at birth—forces that would control the future life of the infant—seems to run counter to common sense. Radiative effects are also dubious. It is even less likely that the stars—each one a sun in its own right and several hundred thousand or more times farther from the earth than our sun—would exercise critical effects on a baby at birth. Some seasonal effects there might well be, for a baby born in northern latitudes in April faces initially a warm summer period; one born in October, a cool winter season.

Before the days of modern astronomy, it made sense to look into possible justifications for astrological beliefs, but it is silly to do so now that we have a fair picture of man's place in the universe.

HOROSCOPES: THEIR PREPARATION AND INTERPRETATION

Astrology claims to foretell the future by studying the positions of the sun, moon, and planets in relation to the constellations of stars along the celestial zodiac at the time of the birth of the subject. This is done through the medium of the *horoscope*. Anyone with a knowledge of beginning astronomy and with an American Nautical Almanac on his desk can proceed to draw one. I have found it a not unpleasant pastime on several occasions. Some of our readers may be interested in learning a little about the technical procedures involved in the preparation of a horoscope. Figures 1 and 2 may help to illustrate the procedures.

For a given place on earth—the birthplace of the subject— the celestial sphere is drawn in the standard manner favored by teachers of college beginning-astronomy courses. We see in figure 1 that the local celestial meridian (a great circle passing through the celestial poles, the zenith, and the north and south points on the horizon) and the local celestial horizon (the great circle 90 degrees away from the zenith overhead) divide the sphere into four equal parts. The celestial sphere is further divided by cutting each of the four sections into three equal slices by great circles passing through the north and south points on the local horizon. The ecliptic, which traces the sun's annual path across the sky, is just as it would have been observed at the time and place of birth. The celestial equator at the time and place of birth is also shown, but it plays a small role in horoscope preparation, helping only to plot the position of the sun, moon, and planets from the Almanac. The intersections between the twelve great circles and

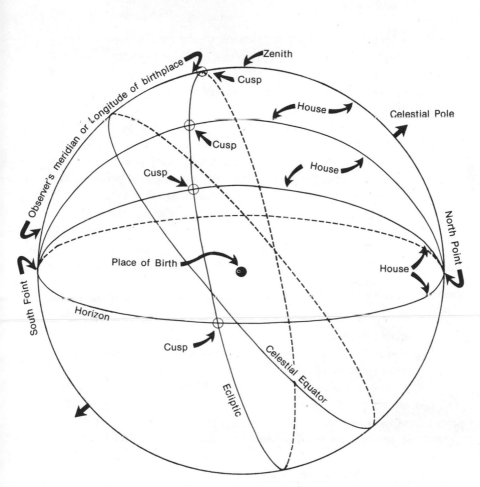

FIGURE 1: THE CELESTIAL SPHERE DIVIDED INTO TWELVE PARTS.

the ecliptic circle mark the *cusps* of the twelve *houses*.

We are now ready to draw the horoscope for the subject at the time and place of birth. We see in figure 2 that the houses and their cusps are drawn on a graph representing the plane of the ecliptic. This is accomplished either with the aid of suitable astrological tables or by the use of some simple spherical trigonometry. The whole business can, if one desires, be prepared nicely as a program for a reasonably fast computer. All of these facts help create the impression that astrology is basically scientific in nature. The houses are numbered from 1 to 12 (as in figure 2), with house 1 being the one that is about to rise above the local horizon. Standard tables are then used to mark the positions of the zodiacal constellations in the outer margin of the horoscope wheel. The positions of the sun, moon, and planets are shown by their symbols in the houses where they belong.

To sum up: Figure 2 shows a horoscope in which the twelve houses, with their cusps marked, and the positions of the zodiacal constellations and the sun, moon, and planets are drawn on the plane of the ecliptic, just as they would have been observed at the time and place of birth of the subject.

The type of horoscope shown in figure 2 is a *natal* horoscope. It becomes—according to astrologers—the all-important guide to predicting a person's future. There are other types of horoscopes in use—*judicial* and *hororary* ones, for example—but these need not concern us here.

The abracadabra begins when the astrologer starts to interpret a person's horoscope. The first and most important item is the date of birth, which makes a person an Aries if born between March 21 and April 19, a Taurus if born in the month following, and so on. The date of birth, naturally, fixes the sign of the zodiac in which the sun is located. It is the important fact that tells whether a person is an Aries, a Pisces, or whatever.

FIGURE 2: A CONVENTIONAL TYPE OF NATAL HOROSCOPE.

The horoscope is drawn for November 23, 1907, 4 a.m. Eastern-Standard Time, latitude 40°43'N, longitude 73"58'W. The spokes of the wheel mark the limits of the houses; the zodiacal signs and the degrees mark the cusps. The position of the sun, moon, and planets are shown by their symbols.

The next important item to note is if the moon or sun is in the first house—the one that is about to rise above the horizon at the time and place of birth—and what planets are there. The *ascendant* is defined as the sign of the zodiac that is associated with the first house. It is obvious that the time of birth must be precisely known if a proper horoscope is to be prepared.

Third in line are the positions relative to each other of the sun, moon, and planets in the various houses. The so-called *aspects* are noted. These indicate which celestial objects are in conjunction (near to each other in position), and which are 60, 90, 120, or 180 degrees apart in the heavens. These aspects are important for astrological interpretation, as are the positions of the planets in the houses in which they are found.

The astrologer can refine his interpretations to any desired extent—the end product becoming increasingly more expensive as further items are added.

How and by whom were these rules of analysis and interpretation of horoscopes first established? They go back to antiquity, basically to the work of Ptolemy in the second century. Ptolemy wrote two famous books: *Almagest,* the most complete volume on the motions of the planets published during the great days of Greek astronomy, and *Tetrabiblos*, the bible of astrology. The *Almagest* is today treated with respect and admiration by historians of science, and it is clearly one of the great works of the past. However, no astronomer would think of referring to it today when considering problems related to the motions of the planets. *Tetrabiblos* is still the standard reference guide for the astrologer. Astronomy has been a constantly changing and advancing science, whereas astrology has essentially stood still since the days of Ptolemy, in spite of tremendous advances in our knowledge of the solar system and the universe of stars and galaxies.

A SCIENTIST'S VIEW OF ASTROLOGY

I continue to ask myself why people believe in astrology. I have asked this same question of many who apparently accept its predictions, including some of my young students in beginning astronomy courses. One answer is simple and straightforward: "It would be nice to know what the future holds; so why not consult astrological predictions?" In addition, some people feel that it is useful to have available certain impersonal rules by which to make personal decisions. Astrology does provide reasonably definite answers and does yield firm guidelines for personal decisions. Many people find this very comforting indeed.

Believers in astrology have a remarkable faculty for remembering when predictions come true and ignoring the occasions when the opposite is the case. And when failure of a prediction does stare us in the face, the astrologer who made the prediction can always get out of trouble by citing the famous dictum that the stars *incline* but do not *compel.*

I have learned that many people who take astrology seriously were first attracted to the field by their reading of the regular columns in the newspapers. It is deplorable that so many newspapers now print this daily nonsense. At the start the regular reading is sort of a fun game, but it often ends up as a business. The steady and ready availability of astrological predictions can over many years have insidious influences on a person's personal judgment.

For some people astrology has become a religion. I urge them to examine their beliefs with care. At best, astrology can be looked upon as a self-centered approach to religious beliefs, for it deals primarily with daily affairs and with what is best for a particular person. Astrology, when practiced as completely as possible, takes away from each of us our right and duty to make our own personal decisions.

The most complete religious approach is found in people who have "experienced" astrology, who deep inside themselves "know" astrology to be true, and who believe profoundly in the effects of cosmic rhythms and "vibrations." I do not know how to convince these people that they are on the wrong track, and hence they will have to go their chosen ways.

Many believers in astrology speak glibly of the forces exerted by the sun, moon, and planets. I should mention here that these forces—according to astrology, critically effective only at the precise moment of birth—can hardly be gravitational or radiative in nature. The known forces that the planets exert on a child at the time of birth are unbelievably small. The gravitational forces at birth produced by the doctor and nurse and by the furniture in the delivery room far outweigh the celestial forces. And the stars are so far away from the sun and earth that their gravitational, magnetic, and other effects are negligible. Radiative effects are sometimes suggested as doing the job. First of all, the walls of the delivery room shield us effectively from many known radiations. And, second, we should bear in mind that our sun is a constantly varying source of radiation, radiating at many different wavelengths variations that are by themselves far in excess of the radiation received from the moon and all the planets together.

Many believers in astrology have suggested that each planet issues a different variety of special, as-yet-undetected radiations or "vibrations" and that it is the interplay between these mysterious forces, or quantities, that produces strong effects of an astrological nature. If there is one thing that we have learned over the past fifty years, it is that there is apparently conclusive evidence that the sun, moon, planets, and stars are all made of the same stuff, varieties and combinations of atomic particles and molecules, all governed by uniform laws of physics. We have seen samples of the moon that are similar to rocks on earth, and as a result of our space probes we have been able to study the properties of samples from the surface of Mars. It seems inconceivable that Mars and the moon could produce mysterious waves, or vibrations, that could affect our personalities in completely different ways. It does not make sense to suppose that the various planets and the moon, all with rather similar physical properties, could manage to affect human affairs in totally dissimilar fashions.

There are many other questions that we can ask of the astrologers. For example, why should the precise moment of birth be *the* critical instant in a person's life? Is the instant of conception not basically a more drastic event than the precise moment when the umbilical cord is severed? Would one not expect to find in human beings the same cumulative effects that we associate with growth and environment in plants and animals? Astrology demands the existence of totally unimaginable mechanisms of force and action.

I shall not deal here with statistical tests of astrological predictions or with correlations, since Lawrence Jerome covers this topic in his article. At one time I thought seriously of becoming personally involved in statistical tests of astrological predictions, but I abandoned this plan as a waste of time unless someone could first show me that there was some sort of physical foundation for astrology.

What specifically can astronomers and scientists in related fields do to make people realize that astrology is totally lacking in a proper scientific foundation? Speaking out firmly whenever the occasion demands is one way to approach the problem. This is the course that I have steadily pursued, and I hope that astronomers, young and old, will follow me on this path. I have frequently recommended that there be one or two lectures on astrology, somewhat along the lines of this essay, in each introductory astronomy course. The students should feel free to bring their questions to the instructor. An interesting experiment has been undertaken in the Natural Science 9 course at Harvard University in which the instructor, Michael Zeilik, is teaching a section called "Astrology—The Space Age Science?" that involves among other things a laboratory exercise in which natal horoscopes are cast.

The fact that some recent textbooks on astronomy contain sections (or chapters) on astrology is a most encouraging development, as is a chapter on the subject in George Abell's book *Exploring the Universe* (third edition, 1974). I have read a similar chapter in an introductory astronomy textbook now in preparation. Let us have more of this!

THE PSYCHOLOGY OF BELIEF IN ASTROLOGY

Thirty-five years ago, my good friend and colleague at Harvard University, the late Gordon W. Allport, one of the finest psychologists of his day, drafted at my request a brief entitled "Psychologists State Their Views on Astrology." The executive council of the Society for Psychological Study of Social Issues endorsed this statement, which was publicly released. I wish to close this essay by reproducing it once again.

> Psychologists find no evidence that astrology is of any value whatsoever as an indicator of past, present, or future trends in one's personal life or in one's destiny. Nor is there the slightest ground for believing that social events can be foretold by divinations of the stars. The Society for the Psychological Study of Social Issues therefore deplores the faith of a considerable section of the American public in a magical practice that has no shred of justification in scientific fact.

The principal reason why people turn to astrology and to kindred superstitions is that they lack in their own lives the resources necessary to solve serious personal problems confronting them. Feeling blocked and bewildered they yield to the pleasant suggestion that a golden key is at hand—a simple solution—an ever-present help in time of trouble. This belief is more readily accepted in times of disruption and crisis, when the individual's normal safeguards against gullibility are broken down. When moral habits are weakened by depression or war, bewilderment increases, self-reliance is lessened, and belief in the occult increases.

Faith in astrology or in any other occult practice is harmful insofar as it encourages an unwholesome flight from the persistent problems of real life. Although it is human enough to try to escape from the effort involved in hard thinking and to evade taking responsibility for one's own acts, it does no good to turn to magic and mystery in order to escape misery. Other solutions must be found by people who suffer from the frustrations of poverty, from grief at the death of a loved one, or from fear of economic or personal insecurity.

By offering the public the horoscope as a substitute for honest and sustained thinking, astrologers have been guilty of playing upon the human tendency to take easy rather than difficult paths. Astrologers have done this in spite of the fact that science has denied their claims and in spite of laws in some states forbidding the prophecies of astrology as fraudulent. It is against public interests for astrologers to spread their counsels of flight from reality.

It is unfortunate that in the minds of many people astrology is confused with true science. The result of this confusion is to prevent these people from developing truly scientific habits of thought that would help them understand the natural, social, and psychological factors that are actually influencing their destinies. It is, of course, true that science itself is a long way from a final solution to the social and psychological problems that perplex mankind; but its accomplishments to date clearly indicate that men's destinies are shaped by their own actions in this world. The heavenly bodies may safely be left out of account. Our fates rest not in our stars but in ourselves.

Astrology:
Magic or Science?

Lawrence E. Jerome

Astrology:
Magic or Science?

C an astrology be disproved? Literally thousands of volumes
have been written on the subject over the ages, attacks and
defenses, apologies and interpretations. Proponents have claimed
astrology as a "science" and an "art," a true interpretation of the
inner workings of the universe. Opponents have mostly attacked
astrology on physical grounds, citing the old classical arguments:
the question of twins, the time of birth versus time of conception,
the immense distances to the planets and stars, and so on.

But very few writers have come to the nub of the matter:
astrology is false because it is a system of magic, based on the

magical "principle of correspondences." In fact, astrology—or at least its prehistoric predecessor—probably arose concurrently with the magical world view of early civilized man, astrology and magic adding to each other and being developed and used by the priests to lend "cohesiveness" to the evolving city-states. By the time cuneiform and hieroglyphic writing had been developed, astrology in some form or other was already a part of man's culture.

Thus, several thousand years have gone into the development of astrology, into its theory and practice. Astrology proper began in Babylonia as a system of omen-reading to foretell the fate of kings and realms. More or less simultaneously, the Egyptians developed their system of Places, based on "planetary aspects." Then the Greeks took over both the Babylonian and Egyptian systems, combining them into a complex mathematical cosmology. Under the Greeks, astrology became available to the common man; astrologers today use virtually the same system as the Greeks, or endless variations thereof.

As a result of astrology's long history, confused development, and obscured theoretical bases, it is common for writers and astrologers to state that the ancient "art" cannot be disproved, that modern man lacks the necessary "cosmic insights" to grasp its truths. Even the great humanist Petrarch attacked astrology only by making fun of astrologers, leaving the cosmological arguments relatively untouched. Very few writers indeed have associated astrology with its magical bases; a reasonable search reveals that only Isidore of Seville, in the seventh century, and recently Richard Cavendish, in *The Black Arts* (1967), have properly identified astrology as magic.

This confused state of affairs is precisely the astrologers' aim: as long as they can obscure the fact that astrology is nothing more nor less than magic and totally unrelated to physical science, they can continue to find customers willing to part with hard-earned funds. For, after all, astrology *is* a practical "art"; it has provided many an astrologer with a lifelong living.

The purpose of this article, then, is to try to provide that "final disproof" of astrology. The plan is simple: I shall demonstrate that astrology arose as magic and that physical arguments and explanations for astrology were only attempts to associate the ancient "art" with each important new science that came along.

First, I shall trace with Alexander Marshack the prehistoric origins of astrology in lunar notations and ritual timekeeping, which suggest that astronomy (the physical observation of the sky) came first and that astrology arose as part of prehistoric and early civilized man's magical world view. I shall prove that astrology is magic because its interpretations are based on the "principle of correspondences," the very basic law of magic. I shall show that it was not until the Greeks—and then later in the Renaissance— that astrology began to be ascribed to physical influences of the stars, long after their magical characteristics had been established.

In the section entitled "The Magic in Daily Horoscopes," I shall demonstrate how the magical "principle of correspondences" is still used by astrologers in making their forecasts. Finally, I shall show that the new scientific field of biological clocks does not provide any support for astrology and that modern statistical studies have likewise failed to discover any direct influences of the heavens on life here on earth.

SEASONAL TIMEKEEPING

Prehistoric man—and specifically the Upper Paleolithic cultures —painted images of animals on the walls of caves; he also carved and formed similar hand-held images, often in conjunction with carved notations, a series of nicks and lines. In "Lunar Notations on Upper Paleolithic Remains" (*Science,* Nov. 6, 1964) and later in *The Roots of Civilization* (1972), Marshack introduced the revolutionary idea that such Upper Paleolithic notations do not represent "hunting tallies" but rather lunar observations, a seasonal timekeeping that aided prehistoric man in keeping track of the seasonal activities of his prey.

Certainly, such seasonal timekeeping would have been of great selective value, permitting man to use his rapidly evolving cognitive powers to anticipate and prepare for the coming hunts. While Marshack tends to place religious and ritual significance on such seasonal notations, one might suggest that the rituals were more in the form of learning and preparation experiences than religious in nature, particularly at first. Play-learning is very common in mammals, especially among the primates; hence, one suspects that ritual play-learning came first and that it was only with the rise of civilization that religion and the magical world view came into being.

Marshack's sequences of lunar notation then further suggest that the traditionally accepted view that astronomy arose from astrology is wrong. It would seem that prehistoric man was making careful observations of the night sky long before astrology entered the picture; plus, he was putting those astronomical observations to a practical use: keeping track of the seasonal comings and goings of the plants and animals that were important to him. In that sense, prehistoric man was far more scientific than the modern astrologer.

Marshack's thesis concerning prehistoric man's use of lunar notation has been generally accepted by anthropologists. The Paleolithic use of linear notation in conjunction with artistic representation goes far toward paving the way for the civilized development of cuneiform and hieroglyphic writing.

Similarly, the use of such linear notations to keep track of the phases of the moon goes far toward explaining why astrology, in one form or other, arose nearly simultaneously all over the globe (China, India, Egypt, Babylonia, Central America). Prehistoric man had been used to watching the comings and goings of the heavenly bodies, and when the magical world picture arose with the advent of civilization, astrology was a natural consequence.

The association of lunar notations with the seasonal advent of certain plants and animals also helps explain why abstractly shaped constellations have animals' names: there was a long history of associating celestial objects with animal life. A similar idea is expressed by Rupert Gleadow in *The Origin of the Zodiac* (1968).

This transition from lunar-seasonal notations to the astrologer's magical horoscope is illustrated in figure 1.

One may well ask, Why would magic develop along with civilization? As in the case of lunar notation and seasonal time-keeping, one can only suggest that magic arose because it was of selective advantage. Perhaps magic gave the burgeoning city-states cohesiveness; one could easily make a case for magic being the power yielded by the priests to keep the citizens in line, convincing them that only by working for the good of the state could they keep the "powers of nature" in check.

This interpretation would further suggest to a hard-core skeptic that civilization does not have a rational basis, but rather an irrational basis of *selective* value—irrational at least in terms of the twentieth century. For magic is based on the "principle of analogies," or the "law of correspondences," as it is generally called in astrology. As we shall see, this "principle of correspondences" is merely a product of the human mind and has no physical basis in fact.

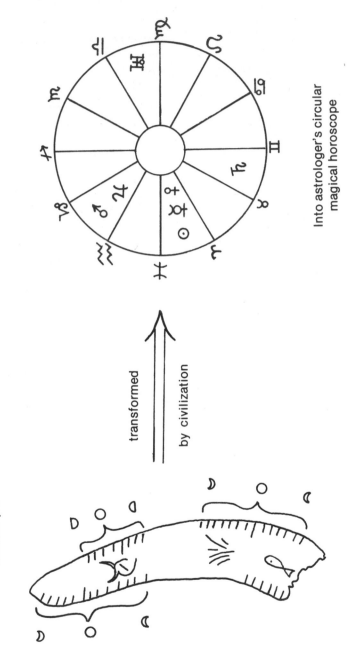

Figure 1: Upper Paleolithic notations on bone become transformed via the process of civilization and the advent of magic into the astrologer's horoscope.

Marshack's prehistoric linear lunar seasonal notations

transformed

by civilization

Into astrologer's circular magical horoscope

THE DEVELOPMENT OF ASTROLOGY

Babylonian priests were quite "skilled" in using omens to foretell future events, usually in reference to business of state. Entrails of animals and natural events such as comets and eclipses were the omen-reader's stock-in-trade. Complex rules were developed for reading the "signs," based upon the idea that if the priest could see some sort of connection or analogy between the omen and the real world, the state or condition of the omen would by analogy foretell the upcoming state of the world.

This is, of course, magic, and it may be fairly stated that essentially all magic—white, black, or sympathetic—works in theory the same way, via the "principle of analogies or correspondences." Figure 2 illustrates the principle: The omen or magic object has certain physical properties that are related to the external world by analogy. For instance, the reddish color of the planet Mars means to the astrologer that it is magically related with blood, war, and the metal iron, which proved so superior to bronze for weapons. The Pisces/water correspondence illustrated in figure 2 works in the same way.

The "principle of correspondences" is fully discussed in Cavendish's *The Black Arts,* Jack Lindsay's *Origins of Astrology* (1971), and my article "Astrology and Modern Science: A Critical Analysis" (*Leonardo* 6 [1973]). Initially, the correspondence is made within the magician's mind by means of his imagination and has only a superficial basis in reality. In most sympathetic magic, the magician's strength of will is supposed to complete the magic link between amulet and corresponding object; only in astrology is the magical link made automatically through the "celestial harmonies of the spheres."

Babylonian astrology was thus very primitive. A strong magical system of correspondences was developed, linking heaven and

Figure 2: The "principle of correspondences," basis of all magic, including astrology.

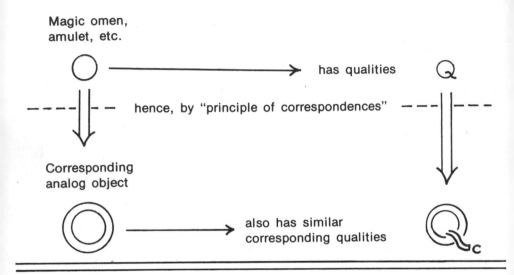

Magic omen,
amulet, etc.

○ ——————————————→ has qualities

hence, by "principle of correspondences"

Corresponding
analog object

◎ ——————————→ also has similar
corresponding qualities

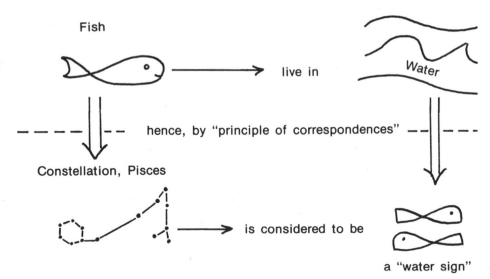

For instance, in astrology,

Fish

——————→ live in   Water

hence, by "principle of correspondences"

Constellation, Pisces

——→ is considered to be

a "water sign"

earth; it was this magical world view that was taken over by the Greeks and mathematically developed into Aristotle's cosmology and what we know today as astrology. The Babylonians were practical people, interested in learning from their omens the tides of war and the coming of the floods so necessary for their agriculture. The Greeks were trying to build up a mathematical picture of the cosmos as a whole and for that reason are considered the forerunners of science.

But Greek astrology was *not* a science. Astrology came to the Greeks as a full-blown magical system, its assumptions and operating principles unquestioned. The Greeks wove astrology into their "scientific" cosmology, setting the pattern for astrologers to attach their "art" onto each new up-and-coming science, more and more ascribing astrology to physical influences and obscuring the magical principles upon which it was based.

Thus, Greek astrology used the same magical "principle of correspondences," adding the characteristics of their native gods to the planets and stars. Astrologers have long claimed that the characteristic influences of the stars were determined through patient observation over many centuries. This is totally false; the astrological nature of the signs and planets is determined strictly on the basis of their magical correspondences. Thus, Pisces (the Fish) is called a water sign, red Mars is associated with war, quick and elusive Mercury governs the metal quicksilver (mercury), planets in opposition are in disharmony, and so on.

As already mentioned, it was the Egyptians who contributed planetary aspects (system of Places): the idea that planets at particular angles (opposition, square, trine) represent omens foretelling events on earth. The Greeks merely superimposed the Egyptian system of Places on the Babylonian zodiac (way of Anu) to come up with what we know today as astrology.

Adding to the confusion between the physical science of

astronomy and the magical practice of astrology, the Greeks used the two terms *astrologia* and *astronomia* almost interchangeably. For instance, Plato uses only *astronomia*; Aristotle, *astrologia*. It was only after astrology became firmly established (by the third or second century B.C.) that a distinction was gradually drawn between the mathematical/observational aspects and their application to predictions.

Astrology, of course, was assimilated by the Romans from the Greeks, and it was in the provincial city of Alexandria that Ptolemy wrote his *Tetrabiblos*, recognizing the problem of precession and setting up the system of Houses still used by astrologers today. (Precession is the slow rotation of the earth's axis every twenty-five thousand years, causing the stars to slowly change their positions in the sky so that the sun during the spring equinox no longer appears in Aries as it did in Hippocrates' time; the astrologers' system of Houses, then, represents the sky as it appeared two thousand years ago, not as it appears today.)

Ptolemy's innovation notwithstanding, astrology is seen to be a system of magic. It fails not because of any inherent inaccuracies due to precession or lack of exact knowledge concerning time of birth or conception, but rather because its interpretations and predictions are grounded in the ancients' magical world view.

ASTROLOGY ALIGNS WITH THE PHYSICAL SCIENCES

Astrology has been called the "durable pseudoscience"—and with good reason. Proponents of astrology have consistently attached their "art" to every appropriate new physical science that has come along, ranging from Aristotle's cosmology to seventeenth- and eighteenth-century astronomy to today's biological clocks. Thus they have been able to preserve their "art"—and their customers.

Aristotle's cosmology is not really a science as we know it, but an attempt to codify what the ancients knew about the universe. Not surprisingly, Aristotle's cosmology differed little from the magical world view then held; he affirmed that the cosmos is a unity linked to a man's soul and that the motions of the stars determine the nature of that soul. His predecessor Plato was a firm believer in astrology, and Ptolemy—writing in the second century A.D.—was easily able to align astrology with Aristotelian "science." All three were favorite sources for the astrologers of the Renaissance in their battles to reinstate the ancient "art."

During the Dark Ages, astrology virtually disappeared, especially after Saint Augustine banned it from the Roman Empire. For eight centuries, Europeans relied on religion and their native superstitions for protection from the "forces of nature." Slowly, however, astrological ideas began creeping in from Arabia, where Greek cosmology and mathematics had taken fertile root.

By the twelfth century, astrology was already well on its way toward capturing the superstitious minds of medieval Europe. The major stumbling block was the Church, which officially frowned on all forms of magic as cavorting with devils.

So astrology was known as a diabolical art to medieval Europe—sensibly enough, since it *is* a system of magic. However, the introduction of Aristotelian science and Arabian astrology tipped the scale back in favor of the ancient "art." The logic and mathematical precision of the Arabian astrological "science" disarmed the distrust of the Church; to the medieval mind, Plato's "harmonies of the spheres" was a romantic and fascinating concept, and it naturally jibed with the ongoing magical world view (which the Church was either unwilling or unable to dislodge).

With the advent of the Renaissance, astrology once again enjoyed a favorable period, much as during the Roman Empire.

Kings dared not be found without their court astrologer; merchants and laborers alike resorted to lucky astrological talismans; housewives and farmers consulted their almanacs.

Astrology became acceptable as a "science" during the Renaissance. Astronomy—which had fared reasonably well during the Dark Ages—became once again merely the observational aspect of astrology. Even Johannes Kepler, who formulated the planetary laws that later led to Newton's discovery of gravity, was employed as an astrologer and dared say little against the ancient "art." (Contrary to Arthur Koestler's claims in *The Sleepwalkers* [1963], Kepler did not blindly stumble upon his planetary laws in the course of astrological computation but rather used his position as an astrologer strictly as a means of earning a living and supporting his astronomical observations.)

When the Copernican theory displaced the earth from the center of the universe, astrology was dealt a serious blow, since it is a geocentric system. Undaunted, astrologers merely shifted their frame of reference from a stationary earth about which the heavens rotate to one in which the heavens rotate and revolve with the earth.

But as the astronomical realities of the universe became clearer, astrology suffered and declined. It became harder and harder for people to accept the notion that heavenly bodies many millions of miles away could influence life here on earth. The immense distances of the stars, the discovery of new planets, the vast emptiness of space, all helped to relegate astrology to its proper realm of magical superstition.

Modern science had arrived to stay.

THE MAGIC IN DAILY HOROSCOPES

Modern science may have arrived, but magic is still with us in the

TABLE 1

Selected Daily Horoscopes Illustrating How the Magical
"Principle of Correspondences" Provides Planetary
"Influences" (to be used in conjunction with table 2—
phrases illustrating correspondences are in italics)

Capricorn, Nov. 5, 1973 (Jupiter in Capricorn): *Especially favored* now: educational pursuits, travel, research. *Achievement* is possible in out-of-the-ordinary ways and places.

Leo, Oct. 8, 1973 (no particular planetary aspects): A day when your *innate agressiveness* will pay off. Energy and drive will finally *bring you* some long-waited *cooperation*.

Aries, June 17, 1975 (Mercury in Aries): Those who are *diametrically opposed* to *your way of doing things* should have your methods thoroughly explained.

Gemini, Oct. 8, 1973 (Saturn in Gemini): *Keep eyes open* now. A *crafty* co-worker may try to shove his responsibilities on you.

Pisces, June 18, 1975 (Mars, Jupiter in Pisces): *Good* day to handle important *obligations efficiently* and make collections. Find the right way to have true *rapport with mate*.

Taurus, Oct. 8, 1973 (Venus in opposition): *Emotions* could get out of hand unless you are *determined* to keep them under control.

form of the daily horoscope. These remnants of our ancestors' magical view of the world are so vague, general, and obviously inane that it is difficult to imagine that people actually read and follow the advice therein. Yet we are constantly reminded that even intelligent, educated people find solace and advice in the daily horoscope.

Most people, no doubt, feel that the publication and reading of such drivel is harmless; however—as will be pointed out in the final section—there is a psychological aspect to astrology that may well result in unwanted and unexpected effects on the personality. Consider, for instance, the case of people born under Gemini, whose supposed astrological "influence" results in split personalities. Does it not seem reasonable that *some* Gemini— constantly reminded of their supposed "split nature"—might well be thus edged closer to the brink of schizophrenia?

Or what about the timid person who happens to be an Aries and thus "headstrong, impulsive?" What psychological damage might occur when he tries to live up to his astrological "nature?"

To prove that the astrological "impellings" of the daily horoscopes are magic is difficult, since they are purposely written to be as vague and general as possible. In fact, daily horoscopes rarely even mention stellar or planetary positions, thus disguising the astrological "reasoning" behind their advice.

Table 1 gives six selected readings from a variety of daily horoscopes. The italicized phrases in table 1 illustrate the type of magical "influences" of planetary positions on which the astrologer bases his horoscope. For instance, the first reading for Capricorns, November 5, 1973 (when Jupiter was found in that constellation), demonstrates the "favorable influence" of Jupiter upon the "natural executive" personality of the Capricorn.

Table 2 provides the magical correspondences of the six constellations and five planets found in table 1. The two tables are

TABLE 2

Six Constellations, Five Planets, Their Namesakes and
Astrological "Influences" (to be used in conjunction
with table 1)

Constellation or Planet	Namesake	Astrological "Influences"
Capricorn	Goat/Fish	Tenacious, natural executive
Leo	Lion	Proud, forceful, born leader
Aries	Ram	Headstrong, impulsive
Gemini	Twins	Vacillating, split personality
Pisces	Fish	Fluid, feminine, attracted to sea and alcohol
Taurus	Bull	Plodding, patient, stubborn
Mercury	Messenger of the Gods	Unpredictable, skillfull, deceitful
Venus	Goddess of Love and Beauty	Harmonious, emotional, sensitive, love of beauty
Mars	God of War	Aggressive, impatient, fighting instinct
Jupiter	Ruler of the Gods	Lucky, sincere, strong, handsome
Saturn	Ruler of the Titans	Gloomy, scholarly, punctual

designed to be used in conjunction with each other so that the hidden magical nature of the advice in daily horoscopes can be followed and understood. A little cross-checking between the two tables should make it clear that the astrological advice found in daily horoscopes is nothing more nor less than simpleminded magic and thus should hold no interest for modern, educated man.

One might wonder why otherwise reputable publishers continue to publish astrological horoscopes, books, and magazines. Profit may well be a driving motive; yet one cannot help but feel that if the true magical nature of astrology were more widely known, interest in it would soon die off, on the part of both publishers and readers.

Moreover, astrologers have long argued (falsely, as we have seen) that their "art" is actually a physical science based on observation. Adding to the confusion, they continually claim as evidence for astrology new scientific discoveries (such as biological clocks, which will be discussed in the next section); these claims no doubt help sway many publishers to support the current popularity of astrology. However, as we have seen, all such claims for astrology are false, and hence publishers so swayed are doing their readers a great disservice.

"COSMIC" VERSUS BIOLOGICAL CLOCKS

When astrologers insisted that their "art" was actually based on physical influences by the heavenly bodies, they were not only disguising its magical bases; they were also unwittingly paving the way for later proponents to align astrology with a new, up-and-coming science—the field of biological clocks.

During the eighteenth and nineteenth centuries, the science of astronomy found no evidence of physical influences by the stars

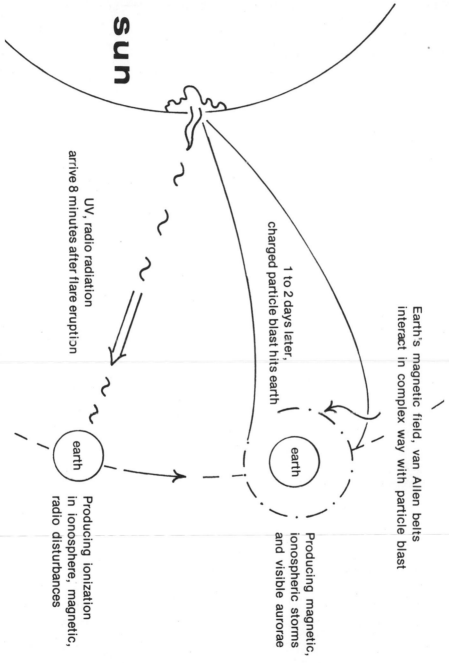

Figure 3: Effects upon the earth of a solar flare eruption.

and planets here on earth, and astrology suffered a decline nearly as great as during the Dark Ages. It was not until the early part of the twentieth century that it was discovered that sunspots *do* have some effect on earth, mainly magnetic and radio disturbances due to ultraviolet and corpuscular radiation effects on the ionosphere sixty miles or so above the earth (see figure 3 for a diagram of sunspot effects upon the earth). There were also hints of correlations between weather and sunspots, as well as sunspot "cycles" in the growth rings of trees and in the economic ups and downs of man; but, as we shall see, these latter findings were mainly due to improper use of statistics.

However, the hints were enough: astrology began another upswing in its fortunes. In 1920, two botanists made the famous discovery that the length of the day determines the time of flowering in plants, and the field of biological clocks came into its own. By the 1950s, it was found that virtually all living organisms display some periodicity, ranging from twenty-four-hour activity cycles to year-long breeding cycles with precise seasonal timing.

Perhaps most suprising was the discovery that both bees and birds possess time-compensated sun-compasses by which they are able to determine direction regardless of the time of day. The mystery of bird migration was fast yielding its secrets to the scientific method: it appeared that birds were able to tell the direction of the sun even on a cloudy day by detecting the direction of polarization of its light. Even more surprising was the finding that warblers—which migrate at night—were similarly able to orient themselves by means of the night sky, again requiring an internal clock to compensate for the earth's rotation.

It was not long before the astrologers were pointing to the field of biological clocks as evidence that life on earth *does* have periodicities corresponding to the comings and goings of the heavenly bodies. Surely, they said, here is proof that the motion of the stars affects life on earth.

Not only do birds migrate by means of the sun and stars, but the Pacific grunion's runs occur in precise synchronicity with lunar tides, and the South Pacific palolo worm rises to the surface of the ocean to breed only during certain full moons. Writers such as Michel Gauquelin, in *The Cosmic Clocks* (1967), and Sheila Ostrander and Lynn Schroeder, in *Astrological Birth Control* (1972), began citing these exciting discoveries about biological clocks as evidence that at least the basic assumption of astrology is true: the heavenly bodies do affect life here on earth.

But as we have seen, such arguments are fallacious, since astrology is based on the magical "principle of correspondences" and not on any supposed physical influences by the planets and stars. The physical-influence argument has been of great help in lending plausibility to astrology where none exists and has no doubt done much to prolong its existence and popularity into the twentieth century.

Proponents of astrology have been aided by an ongoing controversy within the field of biological clocks itself concerning the nature of the clocks. Most of the scientists feel that the evidence points toward biological clocks being run internally and only being triggered by external cycles such as alternating night and day. A few—notably Frank A. Brown and his coworkers—feel that the clocks are being run by "subtle" cosmic forces, much like electric clocks that are run by external alternating electric current. Again, as in the case of sunspot correlations, questions have been raised concerning the statistical evaluation of the evidence supporting the externally-run-clock theory.

In fact, the use of statistics has long been popular with researchers attempting to demonstrate "cosmic influences" on living organisms, ranging from studies of astrology proper to sunspot correlations to studies of "planetary heredity." We shall now take a look at some of these statistical studies, carefully separating the valid from the invalid work and examining the fallacies of the latter.

STATISTICAL ASTROLOGY

A number of researchers have statistically tested the classical astrological aphorisms, and when properly performed, such studies have found absolutely no validity in classical astrology. For instance, James R. Barth and James T. Bennett ("Predicting Human Behavior," *Journal of Irreproducible Results* [June 20, 1973]) tested the claim of an influence of Mars on military careers and found no significant correlation. Similarly, Dr. Bart Bok checked the list of scientists in *American Men of Science* and found the frequencies of birth to be random, once the known seasonal variations were accounted for ("Scientists Look at Astrology," *Scientific Monthly* 52 [March 1941]).

However, when researchers have turned to biological cyclic phenomena, their statistical studies have often yielded somewhat spurious results; cyclic phenomena can be very tricky things indeed. First, we must recognize that there are an almost endless number of astronomical cycles available for comparison: the earth's daily rotation and yearly revolution, the monthly lunar cycle, sideral and synodic periods of revolution for the planets, the sunspot cycles, the sun's twenty-seven-day rotation, and so on. Thus, it is not surprising that almost any earthly cycle can be related to *some* celestial cycle.

The usual method of comparing earthly and celestial cycles is to superimpose curves representing the two cycles: by shifting the two curves with respect to one another, the researcher can usually find some portion of the graph where the two curves seem to match over a considerable number of periods; it is this portion of the graph that usually finds its way into print.

The case of the ecologist who linked the cycles of the Canadian lynx and its prey, the snowshoe rabbit, with the sunspot cycle is instructive. The ecologist analyzed records of the Hudson Bay Company, which had been collecting pelts of the two species since 1735; he found that the two populations fluctuated up and down, displaying a periodicity of approximately ten years. Not surprisingly, the variations in the predatory lynx population tended to follow the ups and downs in the rabbit population with a time lag of a couple of years.

Then the ecologist superimposed the two curves atop a similar graph representing the concurrent sunspot activity: *voilà!* The three cycles approximately coincided over a good portion of their range. The ecologist leaped to the conclusion that the annual fluctuations of the lynx and rabbit populations were controlled by the eleven-year sunspot cycle, a classic example of fallacious deductive reasoning (*post hoc, ergo propter hoc*). While there remains some slight theoretical possibility that sunspots can influence the earth's weather through the ultraviolet and corpuscular eruptions associated with flares (see figure 3), the evidence is extremely weak, and no known chain of causal connection has been shown relating events in the high, thin ionosphere to the weather of our lower atmosphere.

In fact, close examination of the Canadian lynx and sunspot cycles reveals that the correspondence is not really very close. The sunspot cycle is much more irregular, varying from a periodicity of seven to seventeen years, while the periods between lynx maximums only range from eight to twelve years; the two curves are often totally out of phase, sunspot maximums occurring during lynx minimums for the years 1804, 1811, 1860, 1871, and 1923.

Much the same sort of criticism can be leveled at most of the studies relating cyclic biological phenomena with celestial cycles:

unless some known chain of causal events can be demonstrated, the mere coinciding of two cycles does not mean they are related. Moreover, statistics can be easily manipulated (consciously or unconsciously) to yield desired results; the statistical studies of Michel Gauquelin (author of *The Scientific Basis of Astrology, The Cosmic Clocks,* and *Cosmic Influences on Human Behavior*) are a case in point.

Gauquelin began by testing the classical astrological aphorisms and—like the others—found no signficant correlation. However, in the course of his studies, he seemed to find a significant correlation between a person's choice of career and planetary positions at the time of his birth. For instance, Gauquelin found that many scientists were born when Saturn was either just rising or culminating overhead; he found a similar correlation between Jupiter and military men, Mars and doctors, and so on.

Moreover, Gauquelin claimed to have discovered "planetary heredity," that is, his statistics indicated that many people were born when the planets were aligned in the same positions as when their parents were born. Gauquelin has even gone so far as to suggest that women should refuse to take pain-killing and labor-inducing drugs during the final stages of labor so as not to interfere with the "cosmic" moment of birth!

Gauquelin's statistical studies present an interesting case wherein totally fallacious results appear to be scientifically valid; in fact, Gauquelin's research has been checked by several European scientists and statisticians, who could find nothing wrong with his complex statistical manipulations. As frequently happens, however, the fallacy does not lie in his manipulations, but rather in his basic statistical assumptions. As I have shown in a recent publication (*Leonardo* 8 [1975], p. 270), Gauquelin has been improperly applying binomial probability statistics to his data, thus arriving at odds against chance on the order of one hundred thousand to one for statistical fluctuations that are actually well within chance level. (Binomial probability requires one of only two possible outcomes, whereas Gauquelin's professionals can be born in any of twelve astrological sectors—figure 4 illustrates the fallacy.)

Another statistical study of dubious value is Eugene Jonas's research in Czechoslovakia in the mid-sixties on astrological birth control. Dr. Jonas's method is based on the idea that women have a second fertility cycle—independent of the menstrual cycle!— with peak fertility occurring whenever the sun and the moon align at the same angle as at their time of birth. Dr. Jonas's research group, Astra, claimed almost 98 percent success with their birth-control "cosmograms," but careful reading of *Astrological Birth Control,* by Ostrander and Schroeder, reveals the following almost unbelievable discrepancies in the Jonas method: (1) The astrological "cycle" is used in conjunction with the usual "rhythm method." (2) The time of conception is an averaged value based on the weight of the infant. (3) The sex of the child is determined by the astrological "sign" (positive or negative) of the house in which the moon is found (thus based on magic). (4) Test conditions were changed in the middle of Dr. Jonas's large-scale testing of women who answered newspaper ads. (5) Dr. Jonas's astrological computations are riddled with errors.

To sum up, legitimate statistical studies of astrology have found absolutely no correlation between the positions and motions of the celestial bodies and the lives of men. Those studies purporting to demonstrate "planetary heredity" and astrological birth control were either based on fallacious assumptions or were improperly conducted or both. It is not too much to say that such studies are dangerously misleading, especially when the authors recommend that the magic of astrology can replace the knowledge and drugs of medical science.

Figure 4: The fallacy in Gauquelin's binomial statistics.

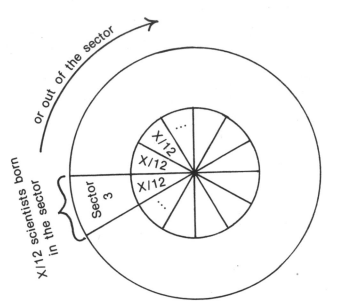

X/12 scientists born
in the sector

or out of the sector

X/12 scientists born in the sector

Sector 3

X/12
X/12
X/12
...
...

To use binomial statistics, he must randomly divide the list of X scientists into 12 and use a different list for each sector.

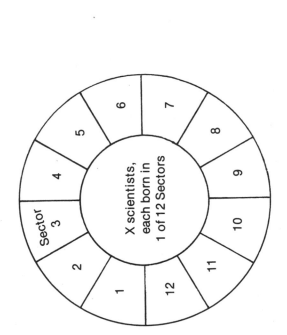

Sector 3

4
5
6
7
8
9
10
11
12
1
2

X scientists, each born in 1 of 12 Sectors

Gauquelin has applied binomial statistics (which require only 1 of 2 possible outcomes) to the total list of X scientists.

"HUMANIST ASTROLOGY"

By far the most esoteric branch of astrology is that which has been misnamed "humanist astrology." Purporting to combine the "holistic" wisdom of the East with the psychology of Carl Jung, "humanist astrology" has been developed and championed mainly by Dane Rudhyar, author of *Astrology of Personality* (1970).

Jung devoted a major part of his psychological studies to the occult; while he occasionally dropped hints that he *might* have thought there was something behind it all, his main interest lay in analyzing the psychology and symbology of the occult, particularly the *I Ching* and astrology. Certainly no other psychologist has gained as deep an understanding of the psychology of occult phenomena; unfortunately, Jung is all too often misunderstood and misinterpreted.

Basically, Jung felt that occult phenomena permit the human psyche to unconsciously express itself through archetypal symbology. In other words, the planets and stars can *only* affect the human psyche through the medium of astrology and its symbols; thus, we might say that astrology *itself* is the influence on the human mind, rather than the traditional view that astrology reveals external celestial influences on man.

Without astrology, there would be no such psychological effects. "Humanist astrology" would have twentieth-century man immerse himself in the archetypal symbology of his ancestors, permitting his psyche to be tossed randomly on the waves of astrological magic.

For those who think that the psychological aspects of magic are harmless, it is wise to point out that magic can and has had profound psychological effect on people, even to the point of causing death within as little as twenty-four hours! To the primitive mind, which believes in magic and its workings, just the verbal hint of a doll stuck through with pins—or Saturn entering Scorpio—may be sufficient to produce illness and even death. As William Seabrook discloses in *Witchcraft: Its Power in the World Today* (1940), magic is *not* a harmless toy. (D. H. Rawcliffe also discusses the dangerous aspects of the occult in *Illusions and Delusions of the Supernatural and the Occult* [1959].)

To be blunt, then, "humanist astrology"—as does all astrology—robs man of his rationality, his most human feature. The astrologer must also face the question of who is to be the master: man's rational mind or his symbolic unconscious.

To bow to the magical "dictates of the stars" is to abandon free will and rationality. This is something the humanist cannot afford to do if he is truly concerned with the good of the human species, especially now amid the complexities of the twentieth century, when man needs all the rationality he can muster.